COLORING IN

Use watercolor brush markers to fill in the open areas of a stamped design…

…or fill in with colored pencils…

…or wet a paintbrush with water and and use it to pull color from a freshly-stamped image to fill in the lines.

MULTI-COLOR STAMPING WITH BRUSH MARKERS

With your lightest-colored marker, color directly onto the rubber surface of the stamp. Working with successively darker colors, cover the surface of the stamp. (By working from light to dark, you can keep your markers from being "polluted" with other colors. If a pen tip does become polluted, clean it by rolling the tip against a wet paper towel.)

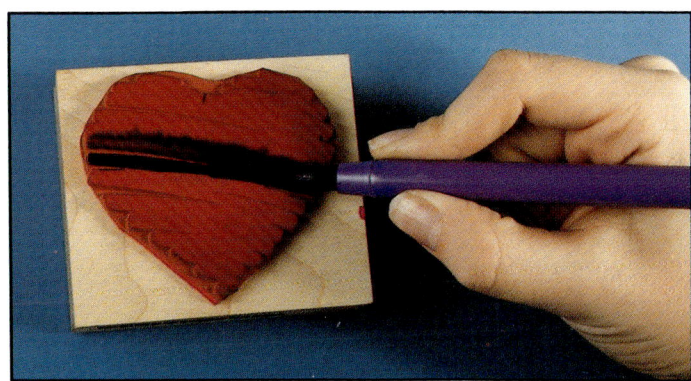

The first colors you applied may dry while you apply other colors. To remoisten, simply hold the stamp near your mouth and exhale on it.

2 REPEATING

One of the most effective uses for rubber stamps is to repeat an image. You can create an effect of depth by using one stamp with lighter to darker shades of the same color.

For example, use the hilltop stamp with the lightest shade of green.

Repeat stamping with one or two darker shades of green.

Next use the wild grass stamp, again stamping in two or three shades of green.

Fill in using a stamping sponge (see page 7) with green and brown.

On this folder, the stamping sponge was also used to create the sky; several bug stamps were used to complete the design.

ROLLER STAMPING

Kids love this—it's fun and easy!

Hold the stamp between your thumb and forefinger. Roll it over the pad until it is entirely inked—be sure the ink is evenly distributed. Press firmly and evenly as you roll the stamp onto the surface—it's easy to press too hard on one side. Practice makes perfect!

Roller-stamped cows border a gift bag.

Roller stamping with fabric ink is wonderful to create special ribbons!

CARTOONING

To streak: Ink the stamp. Press down firmly, then hold the paper still and lift the right edge of the stamp. Drag the stamp to the left for about an inch, then lift it off the paper.

To fade: Ink the stamp. Press down firmly, then lift the stamp. Do not re-ink. Press down again a little bit behind the first impression. Repeat again just behind the second impression. Continue until the ink runs out.

MIRROR IMAGING

Double the size of your stamp collection with Rubber Stampede®'s "mirror image" stamp block! Just ink your stamp and press it onto a clean mirror image block.

original stamped cow

mirror-image cow

Press the mirror image block onto the paper. Hold the paper down as you lift the stamp off.

This card was created with the Cow, Hilltop, Ripple, and Spring Sprigs stamps.

4 USING RAINBOW STAMP PADS

To blend the colors: Tap the rubber stamp onto the pad a number of times, rotating it slightly, which will blend the color on the stamp and the pad. After use, the pad will look soiled, but that's just the blended colors.

ACHIEVING 3-DIMENSIONAL EFFECTS

Stamp the image once onto the final surface, and once onto another piece of paper. Cut out the second image. Bend one or more parts of the cutout upward, leaving a flat area for gluing (in the sample shown, the wing of the butterfly was bent upward, and the body left flat). Attach the flat area of the cutout over the corresponding area of the first image, using glue or double-stick tape.

A flat cutout may be attached with a piece of folded tape or paper, allowing it to float above the surface.

ADDING GLITTER

Use a 2-way glue pen, which has a chisel tip to make fine, thick, or tapered lines. Apply glue to the surface you want to glitter; it will remain tacky until the glitter is placed.

Pour a generous amount of glitter over the glue (work over a clean piece of paper to collect excess glitter). Tap off excess and return it to the bottle.

If the glue pen tip becomes contaminated with glitter, use a razor blade or X-acto® knife to cut a new tip.

MASKING

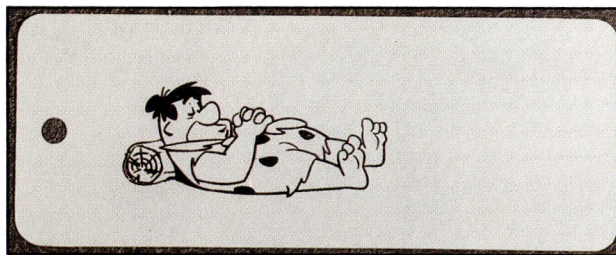

First stamp the image onto the desired surface (left), then stamp the same image as close to the top of a Post-It™ note as possible. Cut out the Post-It™ image, cutting exactly on the outer edge of the stamped lines (right).

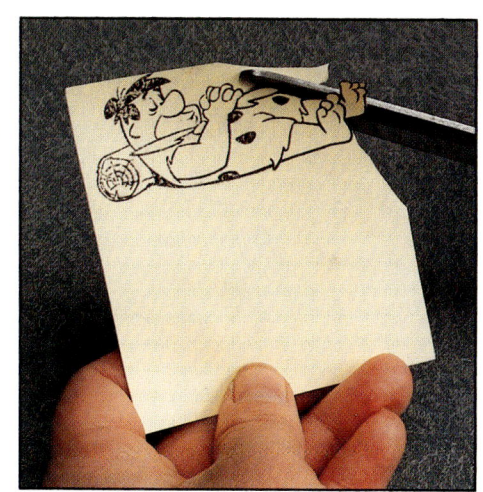

Place the Post-It™ image—the mask—exactly over the first image. You are now ready to stamp background images—in this case, the trees. Stamp them over the mask, which will protect the original image.

When all the background images have been stamped, remove the mask. The original image will appear to be in front of the background stamping. Fred Flintstone was colored in with brush markers to finish this bookmark.

POP-UPS

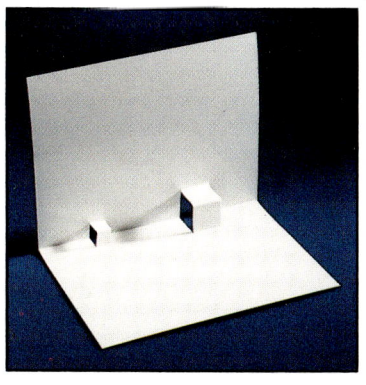

Along the folded edge of a note card, cut two slits of the same length. Open the card and push the cutout area to the inside. Close the card and press to crease the tab. Repeat to make cutouts to support each image you wish to pop up.

Open the card. Stamp and color the desired scene. Stamp and color the images you wish to pop up on a separate card, then cut them out. Use double-stick tape or glue to attach them to the fronts of the pop-up tabs.

In the sample card, Bugs and one palm tree are pop-ups. Two other palm trees were cut out and attached with tape to float (see "Achieving 3-Dimensional Effects, page 4).

6 EMBOSSING

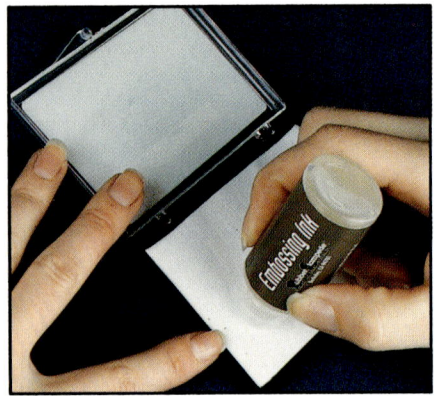

With a rubber stamp and embossing powder, you can create shiny, raised surfaces on paper, metal, glass, wood, leather or fabric. (Embossed fabric will not hold up to everyday wear.)

Apply embossing ink onto the embossing pad. Ink the stamp and apply to the surface. Sprinkle powder generously onto the inked surface, tap excess off onto a card, and return it to the jar. If there is still powder where it isn't supposed to be, remove it with a small paintbrush.

Hold the inked surface near a heat source (heat gun, iron, toaster, 100-watt light bulb, etc.) and watch carefully until the powder melts.

If you wish, color in with markers, pencils, or glitter.

For clear, sparkle, or opalescent powders: The ink color will show through, so ink the stamp first before pressing it onto the embossing pad.

A glue pen or embossing pen may be used to create free-hand designs for use with embossing powders.

STICKER PAPER

Kids can make their own stickers with this glossy paper, which has a crack-and-peel backing. Stamp out the image as usual, cut out, peel off the backing, and stick it on. Overlap images to create dimension.

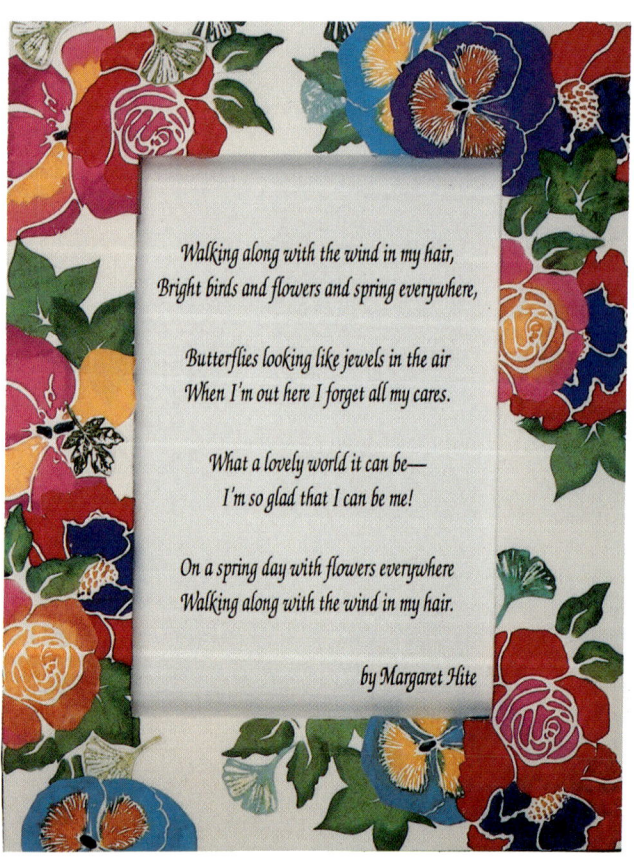

SPONGING TECHNIQUES

Airbrush look: Press a sponge firmly onto a stamp pad, or apply color with a brush marker. Blot the sponge on scratch paper, pressing down several times to clean the ink out of the edges. Press it lightly onto the surface, working from the edges in. Hold the sponge flat for smooth color.

Sponges as brushes: To create a solid field of color, use brush markers to ink one side of the sponge. Don't blot the sponge. Slide the sponge across glossy stamping paper, repeating as necessary for the desired effect—shown at the bottom of this card.

Burst of color: Stamp the image, then cover it with a mask (page 5). Ink a sponge with a marker or stamp pad. Apply ink to only one long edge of the sponge. Tightly pinch the fat end of the sponge on the side opposite the inked edge (left photo). Press the inked edge onto the surface (right photo), pushing the pinched area down firmly over the masked area—it is important that the pressure be over the pinched end, so the sponge contacts the paper lightly at the other end; this creates the tapered point. Repeat around the mask, fanning the lines as shown. Re-ink as needed (you may wish to use more than one color).

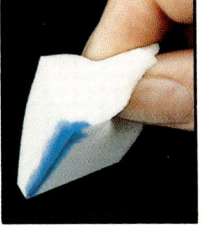

CLAY JEWELRY

Roll clay (Fimo®, Cernit, Creative Paperclay™, etc.) out to about 1/4" thick. Ink a stamp with fabric ink (or leave it un-inked). Press it firmly into the clay. Remove the stamp and cut out the image. Dry according to the clay manufacturer's instructions. Paint if desired, then finish with lacquer or polymer sealer. Add pin backs or other findings.

8 SHRINKABLE PLASTIC JEWELRY

Use shrinkable plastic, such as Shrink-Art™ or Shrinky Dinks™. If it is not pre-sanded, sand with fine (600-grit) sandpaper. Stamp with **fabric** ink pads. Color with pencils, markers, or paint (colors will darken when shrunk).

Cut out. Use a hole punch to make holes for buttons or to attach jewelry findings.

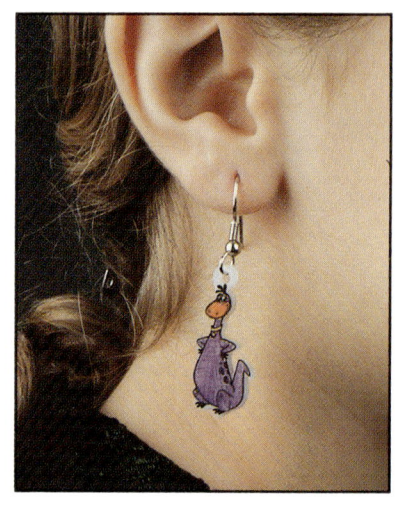

Bake, following the manufacturer's instructions, to shrink the plastic. Allow to cool before attaching jewelry findings.

STAMPING ON FABRIC

Use Rubber Stampede® **fabric** ink pads—no heat setting is required—and smooth fabrics. Pre-wash the fabric. Put a shirt board or plastic-covered cardboard in garments or behind thin fabrics. Fabric inks dry in a couple of minutes and are washable, chlorine-resistant, and non-toxic.

fabric sparkle glue · fabric marker · stamp

Ink the pad; let the ink soak in for a few moments before inking the stamp. Be careful not to get ink on the edges of the stamp. Press firmly onto the fabric. Re-ink the pad every couple of stamps to keep the colors even. Let dry, then color in with fabric markers. Embellish as desired with Rubber Stampede® fabric sparkle glue pens or dimensional fabric paints.

STAMPING ON WOOD

Fabric ink pads are marvelous for wood! The ink is permanent, and there is no need to paint or varnish. Stamp on furniture, boxes, picture frames—use your imagination! Try embossing on wood, too.

For best results, first sand unfinished wood surfaces smooth (the ink may bleed on unfinished surfaces). Stamp as for fabric. The ink will dry in a couple of minutes on unfinished wood; let dry for three to five hours on finished wood. Color with pencils, fabric markers, permanent pens, acrylic paints, or Rubber Stampede® sparkle glue pens.

STICKER IDEAS
Any stamp can be a sticker with Rubber Stampede® sticker papers. Make your own name tags, jar labels, and gift tags—or build a standout sticker collection with one-of-a-kind creations! The glossy paper makes stamp inks and markers look even brighter and more beautiful.

10 LOTS OF CHEER!

A limitless variety can be achieved by combining different techniques.

Instead of ho-hum invitations, why not stamp puzzles? Mail unassembled for your guests to "puzzle over!"

The hummingbird is stamped with a rainbow pad using the fade technique (page 3). The flowers were colored directly onto the stamp with brush markers. Sponging and glitter were also used.

A cellophane goodie bag tied with a bow holds Halloween candies. The star stamps were colored with orange or black markers, and the ghosts were filled in with clear iridescent sparkle glue.

A cut-away card front with stamped fir boughs is decorated with 3-dimensional poinsettias. Another poinsettia is attached to the inside to peep over the front edge.

Multi-colored stamped packages are cut away on three sides to reveal the surprises inside.

FOR YOUR DESK

On the natural canvas of these desk accessories, the stamping has a primitive, irregular character. It is not necessary to use permanent inks, since these pieces will not be washed. Colored pencils and sparkle glue pens were used to accent.

For a very special Shaker box, stamp and emboss the same images on contrasting tissue.

Betty Boop in ancient Greece? Let your imagination inspire you!

Create Post-It™ notes to suit your need of the moment.

WOOD IS GOOD

The birdhouse was painted with ivory acrylic paint, then the "sky" was lightly brushed onto the roof. Stamping was done with permanent inks. Colored pencils and fabric markers were used to color in, as well as to outline some designs.

FOR EASTER

These marvelous eggs were made with the Rubber Stampede® Easter Fun™ Kit, which contains 15 mini stamps and a three-color pad. Some designs were embossed with gold or neon powders (see page 6). The ribbon design was done with a roller stamp and permanent ink. The multi-colored images on the cards were made by coloring directly onto the stamp with brush markers (see page 1).

Stamp this mama and baby with permanent ink, then lightly fill in with white acrylic paint. Dot a meadow with a green fabric marker. Use green and black permanent inks to stamp the leaves and flowers of the border. After filling in with colored pencils, spatter the entire design lightly with white acrylic.

COORDINATED OUTFITS
Stamp a polo shirt with your favorite character, then make shrinkable plastic buttons for it. Add a cap with Mickey and his friends to please your favorite Disney fan.

Temporary tattoos can be made with stamps, too (see Andrea's hand). Just stamp, then color—be sure to use washable child-safe ink pads and waterbased markers.

Stamp a series of shrinkable plastic charms for a bracelet. An extra pair of charms will make dangle earrings, or glue on ear posts. See page 8 for instructions.

MORE FABRIC IDEAS

Pink and perky pigs can help you in the kitchen. The towels and hot pad were stamped with permanent inks, then colored in with fabric markers.

The delicate look of the teddy bear on this jewelry tote was achieved by stamping with permanent ink, then filling in with fabric pencils in coordinating colors.

Glitter glue was added to sparkle the hearts on this pastel pillow.

LET'S PARTY!

The most creative and colorful parties can be carried out with theme stamps—available in a wide range of subjects. You can even stamp on inflated balloons with fabric ink pads! Flintstones and Jetsons cartoon characters were used for the children's party pictured here.